Back to Back
two poets under one roof

Publications by E.L. Freifeld

The Importance of Swimming, Book 1, *1967*
The Importance of Swimming, Book 2, *1968*
Television Analogs, *1969*
Love-Cycles, *1973*
Vermont Haiku, *1979*
Snow and the Study of Trees, *1979*
A Jew in the House of Harvard, *1987*
Poet's Guide to the Holy Land, *1992*
The World According to Animals, *1993*
30 Seconds…of Love, *1996*
77 Sonnets, *1998*
Triptich: Conceptual Poems, *2001*
Wordchess, *2001*
Herbs and Elegies, *2011*
What Walks, [English/Italian], *2012*

Publications by Lois Michal Unger

Miscarriage In Vermont, 1976
The Apple Of His Eye, 1980
White Rain in Jerusalem. 1990
Tomorrow We Play Beersheva, 1992
Poems Political, 1993
The Glass Lies Shattered All Around, 1999
How Country Music Helped Me To Make Aliya. 2012

Lois Unger's poems have been published internationally including Storie Magazine, Italy; Moznaim, Iton 77, Nativ and Arc, Israel. She is a Contributing Editor of Leconte Publications. Her poems have been translated into Hebrew, Italian, Hungarian and Russian.

Back to Back
two poets under one roof

E.L Freifeld

Lois Michal Unger

Edgar & Lenore's Publishing House
Los Angeles 2013

Published by
Edgar & Lenore's Publishing House © 2013

Published in the United States of America

www.edgarallanpoet.com

Cover images are the intellectual property of
E.L. Freifeld & Lois Michal Unger

Library of Congress Cataloging-in-Publication Data
E.L. Freifeld & Lois Michal Unger
Back to Back: Two Poets Under One Roof
Freifeld/Unger – First Edition

ISBN -13: 978-0985471538
ISBN-10: 0985471530
Library of Congress Control Number: 2013917117

Cover design by Apryl Skies

Manufactured in the United States of America
First Edition

FOREWORD

The poems in *Back to Back* are deeply rooted in the kind of life, light and darkness that blooms and sings best in the spaces between the pressed flesh of lovers. The music here is rich, in the moment, on fire with life.

E.L. Freifeld's words fall with an immediacy and no b.s. emotional honesty that brings to mind hard bop jazz as cleansing rain on a lens sharpened by an unflinching mind's eye view of self and surrounding. His work provides a brave new window, open just enough for the reader to slip on through and feel the fresh charge and challenge of the other side. The strange thrill that comes with losing one's self and discovering universal weightlessness tempered with heightened awareness. In other words, a beyond Bloodstone level, natural high.

Lois Michal Unger's words, with their excruciatingly exquisite equipoise of vision and concision, take that window and turn it into mirror with her own starry night— lucid yet intoxicating. Poems true as a well-knit scar that remembers itself every time that hard, clean rain falls. Sometimes it sounds like a round of applause high up on that roof, or a naked 3 a.m. blues, respectful of the pause that bursts with birth—so human it hurts. A place where life expands; where strength and vulnerability work together in sublime symbiosis.

It is in this very place we discover the natural bridge these two souls form when read together. One that can never burn, spanning time and continent. An eclectic, electric main line from Brooklyn to Tel Aviv and all of those soulful, heart food/heartache joints in between.

William Crawford, author of *Actual Tigers* - Edgar & Lenore's Publishing House – 2012 & *Fire in the Marrow* - NeoPoiesis Press 2010

BLACK HOTEL

E.L. FREIFELD

Selected Poems

1996 – 2012

CONTENTS/*Indices*

BLACK HOTEL

POEMS for PEOPLE

STREETS & PANORAMS

MEMORIES OF BROOKLYN

BOMBSHELTER

IT ALL GOES ROUND IN MY HEAD

ABOUT THE AUTHORS

YAHRZEIT
for my brother Bernie,

1935-1989

AN OCEAN A TREE AND A MOON

time and time and time, and time again
until again and again and again
had time become,
there was an ocean a tree and a moon

then came the hand a wrist and a face it
was made that way in bits and pieces,
in picture frames
all in their several places,

like broken people
not altogether young
down to a hair,

nor had the stars broken
nor sun seen anywhere,
but shone

into that tree of childhood ocean,
into that rain the moon had brought
washed our faces and rubbed our hands in the cold,
these were the times from times grow old,

from: *again*
is a mistake time made in my memory

CHICKENS and POTATOES

my mother was born with a sewing machine
attached to her fingers
in a chicken yard, chasing chickens
hid them in the barn when the Cossacks came to town
to kill the Jews
where she met my father sleeping in a barn
found her potato man
on Rivington street too,
circa1922

he'll make a good husband she thought
she knew he'll make due, yes he will

between them i got the best education i can
to know when to dig
and when to 'ran' after chickens
and potatoes

FRIENDLY VISITOR

can you imagine from what distant corner of vast universe
expanding,
came crawling out of black hole of
neutrinos, or where?
passed from star to star
from galaxy to galaxies of milkyway through
rocky asteroids
and cracks of molten meteors
through planets infernos forming, flying walls and
towers of infinity
came

this tiny ant
for this crumb,

fell
from my kitchen table

on the floor

ARROW OF TIME

the arrow of time is the story tells itself
doesn't need air to breathe only space to flutter

invisible wings build wadis
build nations in deserts
blows away in a blast of hot air! in a waft of waves
without a shore,

order follows disorder invisible from within
as before,
love and death play a game called real
stars bloodshot eyes,
from Cupid to Achilles' heal

one tear fills a universe
one grain of sand a sigh,
this arrow of time things grow to love and die
the slower it goes the faster it flies
last always the least,
holding me in your arms when i fall asleep

REVOLVING SOVEREIGNTY OF BIRDS

days of poems and poems of days words
scatter like dust in warm darkness
body sleeps
mind dreams
wakes,
birds gathering crumbs early to rise

see there
the green tail parrots back from their rounds of treetops
crows and mynahs move from day to day
never occupy a single space
just segue

arm in arm,
we walk along the boulevard to the sea
two long tail parrots happily,
turn above the treetops
watch seagulls fly from shores to ships
true lovers
and their kiss

BLACK HOTEL

had i got what i haven't got
i'd probably be dead by now. instead
i'm hole-up in the black hotel
hard to get in, even harder getting out

alone
the world looks all but one darkness to come
i want to shout but merely succumb
i hear murmurs in other rooms
of lover's sighs
of nights lost among the ruins

in the morning
i watch them swoop and gather from my hotel window
step by step they dance down branch by branch
leaves shutter as they advance
down from their highest perch
i talk to them but they only answer in my own words
i study their strange alphabet have not yet deciphered

or paint to palate those murmurs of lovers
nesting under the eaves

MY FRIEND

never a story can be told enough to be retold
they're all so different and alive

a story never grows old or ever dies
and every story is about you

fills the world, and yet
the world is never filled

i'm just a whisper in your ear
a seashell trying to forget the sound of waves
a deep song drowning

oh had we
lived that moment not the next

come then
let me sing your song and tell your story
i know the life you lived in quiet glory

i hear you
i touch your hand my friend,
and our story begins

2ND AVENUE, November

she came floating into my life in one of her private moments
from Lee Strasberg, cruising down 2nd avenue
on her way to the subway
my little bronx gypsy with the green eyes

and when she smiled at my potato kanish
on her macrobiotic diet
i knew all she needed was a hot meal and half a glass of beer

she was my wish come
true she said yes,
dancing in the 'Red Shoes' in her little red dress
up 2nd avenue

we had an argument this morning on who to invite to dinner
for shabbat
after 40 years she threatens to leave me!
where you gonna go i say, back to November?

FOXO/Pan

genetically engineered and fortified with foxo/pan
i bumped into my avatar this morning
on his way back from Mars
where he's been stationed for the past 100yrs
urgently in need of centennial upgrading
just in time for me to disappear
now in, now outside of nature, fin d'siècle
i haven't the slightest idea!

spooks me to think
my avatar has learned to make another me
but delighted to know he can make so many of you
smiling,
and those wonderful happy-go-lucky tits of yours

GOODBYEGUTENBERG

and now, as the sun sinks slowly in the west
let us wave goodbye to our Gutenberg galaxy friends
goodbye Gutenberg galaxy friends
goodbye old book and printed words
as we launch our language of dolphins into deep space,

born in the shadows of nintendo mario and pacman
under the careful scrutiny of play-station
brain re-wired drives hazardous roads
swerving animated,
the gamer generation stalks its enemy
evil empire of fallen angel devil incarnate
marxist manifesto of holograms and virtual reality
trounce unannounced globalism the secret
capitalist wonder on a white horse marches
Birth of a Nation at the end of the movie, have you seen it?

pouncing from cautious pose to aggressive hero
fully costumed
reflex poised on plastic keys a child is born
from heart to fingers
from mind to attack
from living to death
these gamers now texting their epitaph
accelerates news sexting with acronyms
the cold arms of a new friendly game in town

how can we ever understand the strange warmth
the intoxicating vigor the passive spammer
of a true gamer

goodbye Gutenberg galaxy friends, goodbye
goodbye
goodbye,

>52b % 22^ -): hello SIGMA 547

MY APPLE TREE

every moment of her life was accounted for
from 7:15 when she got the kids
ready for school
until 10:35 when she made love to her
husband. the clock runs a jagged course
through dishes and dirty cups
last night's beer and crackers on the floor
straighten the living-room
gather the toys, get ready for bed
no, no, yes, yes.
the supper was fine, who made it?
the coffee was great, who made it?
the house looks good, who cleaned it?
look at my apple tree she says
it's blooming!

SACRED MOMENTS

If you could just *hold on* a little bit longer
it may turn out to be the love of your life
When my father died alone in a hospital and me far away
When i said goodbye to dear friends
because i didn't want to see them grow old
When i made a call i shouldn't have made
When to her I was just a glance, for me it was my whole world
When she said why hang around with people who make you feel bad
When i didn't have enough money to go to my brother's funeral
When my leg shaked that day i thought of jumping off the roof
The here and now was then that never was
The last time i said i love you
The very last moment of my life and you be there
The laughter in the dark the lost in the park
The walk i plan today without waiting for tomorrow
The painful times between two smokes
in a world of sacred cigarettes

ARTLESS

my walk today is brief
i'm sitting on my terrace to catch a breeze
out of the hot sun
i watch the blades of an old air-conditioner downstreet
come dizzily to a halt

i see her each morning fill a cup of water for the crows
perched high on an old TV aerial
legend has it they croak because they're always thirsty
i wonder that they live in deserts and dry cities
her flowers grow red and pink

yesterday that crow flew by my window
and stole a piece of bread
a gray humming bird zipped by the vinkas
paused above the banana tree out back
and disappeared in the bougainvillea

i wonder at the poem of this
how a leaf knows how to pray
to cradle the sun and make my trumpets grow

and so shall i
feel each ripple of unfolding day
replenish the sun, until my seasons run dry
beauty loves to remember and memory hates to fade

was it only yesterday i saw 2 green-tail parrots
nesting in the shade
in that Cedar of Lebanon across the street,
the hum of helicopter troop movements overhead

THE MORNING AFTER

I want to write like a child
but my hand keeps telling me i'm someone else
the leaf trembles because it's a tree
i want to tell you how much i love you
but my mind won't let me

I want to swim the widest sea
a wave is just a child
a caw is just a crow
the ghost of a ship just a seagull

I want to sail in a great ship and see a whale
what is there to know or not to know?
I want to go on a long journey
I want to play with my toys in my car
I want to ask mommy how much longer until we get there?

go back to sleep my darling, it's not far
we'll be there in the morning
when you wake up

HOOKERS

i got a few got away too
that hooker Meg
took me home from Central Park one night
in the dark,

sitting on her bed, took off her shoe,
unrolled her stocking down her leg
remembered what my father said,
jumped out the window i did
and fled

she got away alright, oh Meg
where are you now 'My old Bawd is dead'

then that hook Nancy lived on 10th avenue,
left two kids all day alone
in that fucking dump she called two rooms, a home
found dead in the Village
then came Sue from Scientology, man what she had for free,
cost more than my father's strap, put me on his knee,
you guessed it, she gave me what rhymes with the slap!
or flagella, was it?

but oh i loved them all for free or paid
i can't remember names or even places
Olga, Jill, Denise, Cloris that cunt from Paris,
a kid's gotta get laid,
old men pay twice,
once when they remember
once when they forget the price
put a gun to my head that night they did a
hooker and transvestite in the backseat,
picked'm up downtown Brooklyn in my cab one night
grave-yard shift

got out of that dream just in time
couldn't remember which pocket i hid
couldn't find it almost got killed
that's why i can't go back to sleep again,
ever

plink plunk THELONEOUS MONK

plink plunk
Theloneous Monk
who'da thunk
he thunk of it
always off key, i love it
always unexpect it
thunk you Theloneous
keys pushing back what keeps going down

somewhere in the cosmos there
standing on 8th street and St.Marks
at the 5 Spot,
plink plunk there goes another thunk
rubbing his hands in the cold
to keep his plinkers warm, swaying
for the next set

RED HORSE

whata ya gonna get me for my birthday?
i already told ya kid, a horse, a little red rocking horse
mommy mommy,
whuta ya think he's gonna get me for my birthday
what?
a red horse.

60 score years ago our brother set forth a new epidemic
conceived in bondage and dedicated
to the Afghani proposition you can't refuse,
one score, under devil, dispensable, so help me Lucky
for the junkie, by the junk,
so help me
Lucky.
NY C

fade out:
pan: fade in:

'when i was a kid, every day when i came home from
school my brother wouldn't let me in the house. "Please let
me in, i need the key to the bathroom" in the hall when he
had gone there were a whole lotta burnt matches and
charred spoons left on the kitchen table, and ashtrays full
of cigarette butts. 40 years later he got hit by a garbage
truck with one of those spoons in his pocket, spent
hypodermic and 50cents in small change.
Lucky guy. yeah, right on kids. go for it...'

you got a taste?

when the shit hits the brain pan again, when i am crucified
they will compare me with the worst poets of my times,
down rails of trains and spiders an inch wide (and i don't
mean subway tracks) call me a fascist!
and why you will agree i wanted to kill them all, but still
love me 'cause i said so, and even worse
bit the fucking devil in verse

CIGARETTE #7:

I forgot to count.
we know the time will come
we look at each other
she's playing solitaire
that's what Bronx girls do between dates
as witness, he's writing that she's playing solitaire

the room is full of moments evolving in real time
time is a factor first to arrive and last to factor in
nothing and everything is there

the terrace is another planet
some are seated others floating in thin air
the street, a farther universe

we are watching and waiting for the final madness
to proclaim we are here
all present and unaccounted for...

CHAIM THE BUTCHER

Not all great is the word or vegetable
intellectuals and poets,
the people are greater
we children of the strong and powerful progenitors
workers, builders and butchers

Take Chaim for example,
did you know he cuts a piece of meat as great
as any artist ever ate!
you should be so lucky to met him
would not have starved or vegetate

Stewed, sautéed or strung on shishlik
we stand on the shoulder of Chaim's steak
slaughtered under direct supervision of the rabbinate,
cut to the thick for the pot or ground beef
to perfection

He serves Chaim does, he serves his wife and children
his crazy sons and prolific daughters,
may their husbands live to wake up early and go to work
he serves the hands that will not feed what he has slaughtered
but eat themselves,
the sons too busy to help
the daughters with children have mothered unmarried
the painters and philosophers
the man who washes the floor

Hands soaked in blood, his
children say 'my father
is a meat engineer' or 'beef specialist'
because they are ashamed he's just a Butcher, a shnoder!

I wanted to read this poem to Chaim,
but he said, 'not now, I have no time now. later...'

BAKERY

where i can bake my own bread is a good place to go
cities are filled with stinking manifestos
and incestuous suburban news

i came from the Carpathian mountains
from woods and tribes descended city streets
from streets to rural gangs,
dug their graves so deep no ghosts can tell

we are not made of these and such material
strictly lowercase, the poem writes me
nothing can defeat the tribe but neutralizes
ranges from city to countryside
baking bread and burning charcoal

and in the morning
when light comes streaming through your window
your breakfast of sun is at the door
your loaf of bread is knocking

TOUCH

from whom do we learn but from each other
there is much
in the touch of hands
however brief/in passing/a shoulder brushed on a bus
a few coins exchanged at the toll
what is a brain without a hand to feel a
finger that can do what no tool can
make tools, and according to plan
repair what's broken or cotton to mend

i wonder though that difference discerns a distance
the hand that touched his lover last night
killed 35 Kurdish villagers this morning
seated there at his keyboard,
clicked enter that launched an end to life, of death reaching
sharp fragments of crescent moons from skies fallen
in fresh daylight
fingertips,

(it's that bug in my computer!click 'restore' to 28.12.2011)

I LOVE WOMEN WHO PLAY CELLO

i've been meaning to tell you all these years
i love women who play cello
i never told her, had the chance
i never told a woman i love women who play cello
and why i love them so much

i love women who play cello because they spread their legs
for their instrument
shut their eyes behind spectacles listening
to music we can never hear but playing
those fingers ah those fingers firm
as she plays those lower strings from push to return

she's finished now and lays her cello down
i remove her glasses and see strange chords vibrating
then plays me like her music string and bow
i am her cello now

i would have made a revolution had she but asked, anything
anything to make her music last

MADAGASCAR

Tall monkeys black and white
walk upright in Madagascar
lost continent of the mind,

8 underground volcanoes boil the earth in a pot of dormant sea
lemurs rule and species long untenable
long before you and i
there the world's destiny and tortoises venerable
gods of nature and source of man's instinct, Madagascar
there the ghosts of death and death's eternity

from eastern side to west afar
from dry to wet
there dreams of dolphins fly where harpies nest
there whales of memory spawn their ocean breed
and marvelous insects learn to write and read,
butterflies beetles lacewings spider's university

some things take longer,
build like waves hard leaving what went before
the tides withdrew
to rest among the vines,

until another wave comes washed ashore
until another sky is filled with blue
Tall monkeys black and white
walk upright in Madagascar
waving their arms above their heads
in search of celestial typewriters

MESSINA GATE

it's a toll
a brief walk in the shade
a short rest under a tree
after meat on the fire and a bellyful of flesh
fell fast asleep on the ferry
passed the strait of Messina, then sank

an albatross dropped by for a cup of tea cupping the wind
an amorous moose walked on the back of a whale
the old man saw his wife sinking for the 3rd time
pondered to drown beside her, instead
in a splash
the more she clung the more his arms let loose
or soon they would both be dead!

the tale was the essence of time told a wave on the
sea how would they end together
or separately?

after their nap the wisdom of sleep apparels
a shadow whispered in thin air
you will never know how to love
until you have found someone or something to die for

Le GALAPAGOS

under the blue vertical sun
where pirates come to rest, so do i where
platypus fish and learn to fly where
islands under the volcano are born
where frigate birds float above a blue sea
where the giant tortoise walks slowly over black lava
or ever turns to look
or talk to me,

where iguana fresh water gleans from salt
where finches poke for grubs with little twigs they break
between their beaks

where comes the great whale with his sperm in the spring
where i have nothing to do all day but discourse
with mocking birds in the shade
on the great matter of nothing
with the occurrence of spring

so what am i so self and self imbued more so
than these my brothers and sisters who walk so slow,
how much of less than more i know than these
for thousands of years have walked upon their knees?

Thank you Bishop of Panama
thank you Charlie Darwin for stopping by
what a great place for a man to lie, i can imagine
with my friends and gentle monsters
under a dramatic, National Geographic sky

AYACUCHO

Between the mountain goat and a man is the dream
share the same corner of death
Quechua,
ghosts wandering dismal haze of cold memory
language echoing
descended from the Huari 15 thousand years before the Incas
north of Ayachuco in Pikymachay
hillsides of Andes tribes and flocks ancient

upwind they hunt swoop down on villages
killing all but the woman, take to their bosom
these and more stand firmly at the door of 33 churches now
one for each year of his life and
like all true legion of faith, will die for him!

will you die for your cause
as they for their Christ would live?

Ayacucho,
manco capac, poley campos, abimael guzmán reynoso
surrounded by soldiers (and my friend there to witness)
17 killed on the spot they held,
dreamt the night before this so did happen
to find that hole where ghosts may hideaway
only to be met by a tribe of Incas, waving machetes
sendero luminoso! the shining path
the death march to socialism and decay,
4 stories buried underground in prison for life
without delay,
and all those drugs!

oh had he dreamt he was a goat and not a man
he might have haunted another hole to run
and talk to goats and not to ghosts of men
and their revolutions

SICILIA
Questa poesia è aredaction della precedente poesia Catania

In beautiful Catania, she said
men still tip their hats '*buona sere, come stai bene*!
Gaetano's well heated room,
the old man at his window in the sun
eye under eyelids our presence, and Dom Pietro,
'andare al Mercato in piazza Duomo ottenere
tutto quello che vuoi'

In the arms of mount Aetna
in the effervescent glow of white cloud streaming
from its peak of eternal Snow Queen
shrouded in gray dust,
the town and its people rest firmly in their sealed fate,
virtual ambiance of time and timelessness flows

and no crows!
absolutely no crows to be seen anywhere,
all princes who would be kings buried
since The War of Sicilian Vespers, 1282

Gaetano says the volcano is inactive.
shh, it may wake in a whisper
and flood the town in black pasta

HE WHO SAW EVERYTHING
The Gilgamesh Epic, a new recension

[I]He who saw everything
[I]He who saw everything
from the first to the last
who embarked on a long journey to the underworld
to bring his friend Enkidu back to life who
bent over his friend as over a woman
who built his ship of death and sailed
who crossed the great waters with Urshanabi the boatman
[I]He who saw everything
who embarked on a long journey and returned to his homeland
whose spirit broken has none to take care of him
what was left over in the pot
the pieces of bread that were thrown in the street he eats
[I]He who once ruled the nations who contended with the gods
who killed the terrible Huwawa and beheaded the fierce Humbaba
[I]He who is 3 parts god and 1 part man bi-sexual
[I]He who must die
[I]He who saw everything
now gathers the dust for bricks to lay and sighs among the ruins
rebuilds the temple and counts the number of his days...
[I]He who saw everything
[I]He who saw everything

LAG B'OMER
A Modern Epic

it's a cold wind blows in from the peninsula
the true epic of our century has yet to be written, and for good reason.
shall we once and for all be rid of this albatross?
oh no, no,
like old crows still come to visit new waves
loiter on street lamps lit for moonlight, ships in the night
seasons themselves have altered their course
sun and moon rise in place of each other, apocalyptic!
from the desert to the sea, from ancient Torah
from the word of G-d to modern history, floods
from Jew to Jerusalem
from Nabatian to Plishtim
from Plishtim to Palestinian
because they couldn't pronounce the letter p, to Bedouin
4 tribal dynasties descended: from Rashid
5,000 ex-terminated, from Havitat Bin Laden and the few,
from Ibn Saud Faisal to Mecca megabucks,
from Abdullah 15,000 expelled to Transjordan,
from burning sand to scorched oil,
from desert to sea this nation,
these nations together rise and fall to claim this land

the heart is a lonely scholar, strolls on paper
from sea to desert from desert to sea
fires of Lag B'omer on mount Meron, from Moses to freedom
from Hashem to Jesus, from Jesus to Mohamad,
i walk in the shadow of our fathers.
i am bound as an olive branch to an olive tree
i want to escape but there's no One to comfort me,
from Rashid to Shoar
once my brother as in Torah
now my enemy in the Wadi
unlike those epics of old
from the gardens of Cleopatra at Luxor
of Helen of Troy, of Beatrice and Lenore

from hell to paradise, songs of the troubadours
ours will be an epic of peace in a century of war

m' ha peh sheli le elohim - from your mouth to G-d's ear[1]

---

[1] Lag B'omer is the holiday celebrating the death of Rav Shimon bar Yochi, father of the Kabalah, who fled from Roman persecution and lived in a cave for 19yrs, on Mount Meron. And when he finally emerged, G-d made him go back into his cave for another year to calm his enthusiasm because the light cast from his eyes upon the world, was too intense!

THE SOUL'S RESIDENCE

The soul's residence is the place it dwells
deep or shallow
as alternately follows on dwelt.

the wind and flowers and all things specious
drifts along after-hours boulevards,
a stranded hooker dumped in the middle of nowhere
and only doors that open in a whisper
alone, one night in the darkness abandoned
and no taxi in sight

no,
it blows relentlessly into a tornado
flashing sequence in waves of insurmountable water
breaking before birth, the child in her
by all accounts
simply a heart
at a bus stop,
sitting on a bench waiting to arrive

there is that spirit of place longs for always,
talks about walked about
the fire
the flood
the family
and soul's residence

W. BROADWAY

i loved the old pre-soho,
trucks and loading docks and mafia drug dealers in lofts
full of marijuana - had such a lovely neighborhood fragrance
of Columbian gold so resinous, you could get high
smelling your fingers!
and oh the coke and all the cats
and oh
so long ago…

and though i know that 'long ago' was so for me
this *now* is always there for someone else
each in their progress savors an old street
a cookie a history a registry
a temporary file cannot delete
like spyware memories jealous of our dreams, return again
and again, to shadow the street we walked, cops tailing
as we climbed that flight of stairs
to score from my connection on W.Broadway

i count the steps now
but only my dreams can remember how many

WILLET STREET

he have mapped the streets of his soul
an aerial view with a legend
macro'd in on his brain via satellite
brought to you by cortext close-up shot

mists of time the dark place of it
as he swung left on Willet Street on his way home

there in dim twilight the killer, see him
so fast the youth of silence broken changing
hands money death and the lure of wisdom
old knowledge of heaven and hell
the image fades into cliché
the dream ends in fusions of colorless light
the screen now empty
and another 600 dead around the corner
and my friend a convicted pronoun

the carpeted green tables procure the essence of
pool snooker
plays

the light from within pours like spilt blood out
on the darkened pavement, gently
inviting in

RIVINGTON

as the dream-crow flies
Rivington street is all busy pushcarts of apples
and apples to steal, bustling immigrant Jewish mafia
green horns, fresh tub butter cut from the block

and Joey the magician
and his mom bull dyke Annie,
cigarette dangling off her chin
in bell bottom trousers, worked in Coney Island
and uncle Nate who stole pennies from children's pockets

where there's smoke
love is not always the cure
this poem hardly a pronoun simply procures
it is a fact
the picture
the shot,
strictly lowercase

hey, watch this!
Joey's hands shuffling the deck in the hallway

illuminates

in the dark

a new card trick!

87 SHERIFF STREET

everyone knows those streets their own
you walked as the dream-crow flies
the objective self marks with love
the ship of time and times place

you were a child
you know the name of that street
the poem is heard but not spoken
the voices silent now
a single word would shatter
that day you sat looking out the window
dad bought a brand new car
Constantine the Armenian was jealous
the gypsies tried to steal it but didn't get far
and in the evening you played with your friends
kick-the-can ringelevio, i know
because i was there

darkness once lived in the distance
peopled eye now vacant perceives
street lamps utter a faint glow
the voice trembles in her arms
we drove in the car to Queens
another morning
mommy, how long until we get there?

a turtle in the playground at Masaryk Towers
marks the spot where once lived 87 Sheriff Street
gone now,
children still play

THE AIR IS THICK

the streets are empty
the air is thick with tension
buses stop running
wheels stop turning
birds cough and even children stop crying

the silence ominous as still water
gathers the sea from darkening shore
the world shatters with a boom!

any fool can predict a war
only a wise man can say when peace will come

MAN'S CASTLE[2]

for Lois

born in the 40s
i grew up on reruns of b/w movies from the 30s
4 generations have passed before my eyes
and what i have seen,
now everything i see makes me cry
i wonder if the sky is really blue
i wonder why
i wonder at our lives just passing through
are you thinking of me when i'm thinking of you?
and when i dream...

and if one day these words will say it rightly
just as easily or pass away
go my love, you're tired, go to sleep
i'm here beside you watching
nightly

[2] Man's Castle, 1933 - with Spencer Tracy & Loretta Young

YAHRZEIT - for Bernard Freifeld, 1935-1989

every Jew is born with a rabbi sent by HaShem
because even rabbis have to make a living
but it was hard times,
so my brother Bernie was my first rabbi
because the bathroom was in the hall
and it was too cold to go out at night to pray,
it was our small minion
alone,
hugging in the darkness for warmth, that was all we had

one night my brother found a piece of paper on the floor
a broken pencil and a paint brush
from then on
every night found him painting in the kitchen.
i remember
how cold it was that December, i can still feel it

oh dear brother
of art and wisdom showed me there first light
a candle, a flame huddled together to keep warm
i still hold you
will never let you go, no matter where

i am coming Bernie
soon we will be together again
gazing at the universe across the street,
through frosted window
walking down that road over the bridge
building our house in the woods, just like the dream

see,
i saved a brush for you
and a broken pencil

shall i bring you some canvas?

For LOUIS RAPPAPORT

Gee whiz Louis, how was i to know
an apparition of you would pop-up that way
into my soul,
as i strolled by the cafe where we sat and talked
many years ago, together

i saw you floating transparent that morning
in watercolor soup
into my heart humming,
never believed it could happen, ghost or angel
or was it all just in my head?

i can still write said Louis, but can't figure out
how to read from the dead

Louis,
you had a wonderful mind, a great journalist
truly one of a kind

died long before his time
if time is long enough to honor him
and read his song

THE SALT SEA - yam ha'melach

I'm thinking of moving down to the dead sea
to bury myself like a lost treasure
for someone to find me,
it's already dead so nobody bothers to kill it anymore
with bombs and missiles and skyfire

lowest elevation on earth, yes this earth
as it fizzles, is deep enough not to hurt when it falls
to inhabit, only
sometimes hell needs a haven where nobody cares
no wonder the essenes ran to their caves
to massada and their graves, and to en gedi
the garden reserves
ibex and waterfalls scroll among the wadi
camels, and desert flowers bloom

there's enough room to breathe
the sun's vast bakery fed at night
so hot you can cook an egg at the window
and fry your dreams
in your bed

JUMPING FENCES

every so often you gotta shake up the spirits to get things going
toggle the memories before they make you crazy
from the 1st time i looked at myself in the mirror as a child
i and i knew from the get-go we'd be the best of friends
and only
staring out my window at the backyard and all those fences,

until one day i looked in the mirror and didn't recognize myself
and that was the end of our friendship
and went looking for other friends jumping fences
me and Jimmy. in one yard we found a pile of diving boards
but no swimming pool
in another, old chairs asleep under a tired tree
Heredi Jews celebrating Sukkoth,
a 3 legged cat and her refuse haven, scattered last week's dinner

a world of intriguing leftovers spiced with a dash of unexpected
over these fences, found climbing and jumping, until one day
took a running start, and flew over this big fence on Willet Street
and wouldn't you know
this feakin' vicious black dog bolted fat from out of nowhere
and threatened to rip my leg off. not a moment left to think
and froze!
cold as a popsicle and patently irrelevant
stopped jumping,
and started melting

Annex: 15 06 nix nix, Smokey Stover -
the trick here with memories is that you usually know what to
expect when you've landed on the other side of a fence.
in real-time easy to forget. in death know even less.
from then on i wrapped a piece of meat in my pocket
for the dog
before i went jumping

THE DANCING VIOLIN

life gets old as the soul grows young
wondering how on earth it can be, when jeepers!
there he is
the dancing violin player
riffling strings
prancing on wings divine
so totally, delightfully mad!
shows up in the vegetable market downtown
today,
has a patent on real time…pending

he was a perfect elf
made everyone happy with his riff
all the veggies went fresh
and the hawkers laughed

it was a happy day

DREAM VIRGIN

if i was boy enough then and she
not lying there beneath me, last night
in a dream she returned

i made that final thrust and with my hand
turned all her tears away, after all these years
those many years
children now have done, and rise
to write this poem long before sunrise
what might have happened fifty years ago
in a dark room alone with Aida
and my friend in the bathroom
making love to his girlfriend

and when she cried, i turned to one side
but told my friend to prove i was a man
and not a boy who simply told the truth,
that couldn't can,
and told a lie

MERCURY RISING

i am absolved
i weep at the end of grade B movies/made for tv
the boy is rescued from the covert arms of the bad guy
just in time to miss the helicopter on its way
to witness protection,
a sting. i am absolved.
i feel better about everything now that the bad guy
fell off the roof

the moral universe what's left of it is still intact
the good guys always win their rights to illusions
the movie is great. the bad guys are also good
because the bad guys never learnt to shoot straight
leave a trail of blood wide as the Mississippi
and i alone am escaped to tell thee

'a good leader massacres his own people'[3]

---

[3] from Intimate Journals, by C. Baudalaire

IF I COULD ONLY TELL YOU

If i could only tell you, but no you had to be there
it's a joke which nobody laughs
only it's there belongs to you, not my there, naturally
2 angels wandering the dark streets of
yesterdays looking for the Brooklyn bridge back
to Manhattan if you can read this

i swear it could be anywhere
the kitchen table in dim light the old
ice box my father hugging the radio
listening to the Joe Louis fights,
my brother painting black pictures through the night
it's all there pop in his soft chair
the sofa on which my sister slept for 20yrs
faintly like a calm sea, dimly
watercolors wash drifting
tub in the kitchen bathroom in the hall, dimly
4 rooms railroad flat,
and that wall outside my bedroom window

first time i saw a girl undress lived on the
first floor i still imagine lying down beside
her squint seeing, if at all
a gift of memory, of nostalgia
of cold nights itching
of warm eves shuffling cards in penny poker
after dinner of throwing garbage out the window.

my mother always beat me at chess
my sister took care of me when i had whooping cough
for love of me i can't remember my mother's breast,
now dreaming

AMERICAN MYTH - Joe Palooka

thought he could punch his way to paradise in Las Vegas
buncha palookas
tumbley humpty down poor schmuck
pugnacious Horatio Algers make histories of themselves
climb out of the ghetto to riches from rags
get fat and fuck all the bitches and fags
all you underdogs and have not hads
bark at cauliflower ears
bubble-gum brains American dream benevolent autocrat
cultivating bastard of an old mogul
can't do you anywhere will now abuse
you this electric avenue epitaph

you can't beat the house the house always wins
too big for Washington and New York
too big for Montana and Texas too big
too big for underdog suckers like you and me
too big for a ride home alone on the subway to Palookaville
at 3:00 o'clock in the morning

oh but Joe i love you so
Rocky will put you back together again he owns Las vegas
put a fix in
book a fight at Caesar's Palace and let you slide into home

JAFFA

Jaffa's a tough town,
behind the clock a clan of thieves swarming,
ambles like brambles of gangs libertine
old town port of ancient standing
old drainage needs repair
stroll like rows of fishing boats down to the pier
and the rock of prometheus

in those days when dynamite was used to waken the fish
my friend Yoram blew his hand off up to the wrist

why napoleon came to fish and king arthur
came to fish,
and walk the road to jerusalem and demascus.

Who dredged the swamps and died of malaria?
bones washed ashore
old cobblestone city,
haven of lost souls arabs jews bucharan
french italian german,
where freedom still tries it's trade in the ancient fleamarket
where beggars once princes line the public toilets
daily gathered dirty from the garbage like poems
to take a piss,
what stories what lives what effigies
what hidden treasures buried in that old town
what divine trash of illusions and hallucinations
pouring like blood from the souls of kings
and hearts of old-time hookers,

with a bad day at the market
and nothing to sell

SHUKY Malachi

one of my favorite bums in the shuk is gone!
for 30yrs the toothless old yid slept in his jalopy
sold dirty spoons and forks and rusty tools on broken plates
schmunzas and tchachkelas and other non-descriptive
is gone
can't even remember his name, always asleep in the sun there
under an umbrella, hands folded in his lap
holding a half-eaten cucumber,
you'd have to wake him to pay him for what you took

his name was Malachi, now i remember
a king of the shuk, haven't seen him lately
i hope he's not dead. Malachi was his name
the king is dead
long live the king

though i've committed some crimes in my life,
my soul is spotless
i found it today sitting in Malachi's place
and just as i reached my hand out to take it
someone bought it out from under me!

how much? he said to the two young guys, talks fast
got it for 20 shekels he did
a little bust of Saddam Hussain with a chip on his nose
and a flea in his ear.
what did he kill for less than his share
no more than America?

ah well, nothing is perfectly die at home
never interfere with someone else's buy,
it's fleamarket etiquette. fuck you!
(i offered him 30 shekels, 40 as he walked away
but he wouldn't sell)
i blew it

RED DRESS

among the clocks the lamps and shoes
the old woman with her pile of clothes there
between the plates and old furniture
the cute little red dress she wore when they first met
or was it really hers?
the eye will find among antiquities
all these that waken dreams of days long gone
flickering memories
lights in a harbor
tiny stars barely visible at night

as they grew old together
sitting on a park bench holding hands
he remembered
she was so cute and he so handsome fit
you still have a baby face she said
you know i can't wear those kinds of dresses anymore
you want me to look like lady Gaga!

he smiled and asked how much for the dress
only 5 shekels?

BOILER ROOM GANG

Down in the hull of the phantom ship Seawolf, starring
the great John Garfield nee Julius Garfinkel
is the boiler room gang

these cellar rats and lamesters[4]
these discards, brutes of humanity
born of no common decency but common
matter in the rough for revolutions to come
these marvelous outcast cum-unions of mutiny
and charcoal burners,
underworld of the world all powerful
not just criminals but justice also,
and for the great turning of the wheels of the world
and of the ten lost tribes

what is your race color or creed, just a bunch of gangs
and virtuous thieves.
the moral imperative still reigns
the world is whole,
for the time being

in G-d we trust
E Pluribus
Unum

---

[4] Lamester or 'on the lam'- old slang for gamblers and
welchers who run away from their debts

AGUS

see Agus
Darfur black man or Sudanese
tall as a tree thin as a leafless branch
came to us said he was hungry
speaks ancient language no one understands
see Agus work in the hot sun
works harder than 10 men
and when i pay him
he pulls a tiny purse from his pocket
to put the coin in
for a loaf of bread

shabbat shalom i say to him
shabbat shalom he replies
and i wonder
how many coins will fit in his purse
as i look into his eyes and see centuries of African sunrise

THE DEFINITIVE SNOOKER POEM

it all began with a hole.
unlike Alice, the Queen got tired of playing in the garden
so the king reduced the size of his balls
were once the size of bowling, made circles on the grass
where his Queen could lie on her ass
while rolling a bowl in her hole with a cue
stick of her sensual universal. made sense
first find your hole then fill it with his eminence!

so the game was born Snooker
from ancient times writ
by any other name made oblong first
from a circle to fit, then squared
then doubled the squares
then tabled indoors,
not wanting to drop his balls on the floor, added 6 pockets

so the world was made like a game of billiards
so says Nicolas Cusanus
dubbed it Snooker and proceeded to play
not as for Kings to wile the day on their anus
but for Queens in their nightshade

'Let us to billiards: come, Charmian'
said Cleopatra whenever Antony was away.

thus began the Name of the Rose, of romance and science,
of poetry and prose

TUMBO

i am a piece of forgotten history, but not by all.
not by all.
in my old neighborhood in fact,
Mira Garfinkel still remembers when i put a handful of salt
in her soup, or was it down her back?
Joey told me that day on the stoop we hung out
what she said.
when Mrs Sadofsky pulled down my pants in the boys'
bathroom and spanked me with a broom.
she's probably dead by now but still remembers,
just because

and Tumbo remembers when we swept the baseball park
for nickels after the game, and soda bottles to cash in,
for Coney Island.
and the girls under the boardwalk,
and Jerry's sister who put my little hand down her skirt for a feel
and my face on her tits, in the hall.
she can still recall. oh yes,
they all remember, it's all there,
it's all there in remembering all about me
because i'm some piece of work,
they all remember me
just because

and Lenny, yeah Lenny i almost forgot,
he remembers me too
and i remember him too about what i forgot and still
wonder so there,
that's a lot

THE DAY HAD COME

The day had come to open that box
and read the letter my father gave me before he died
tears poured down like rain,
my heart beat to the brim
my hand trembled like a leaf caught in the wind
as I rounded the corner of the envelope and tore it open:

To my son Lazar,
I want you to know what I have learnt from my life what it was
it's like a dream, it goes fast
Don't take any wooden nickels
Don't go with the whores when they owe you the fare
You can't be too smart
Go to your mother, be a good boy
Don't give all your money to the phone company,
use the public telephones,
Turn off the lights when you don't need them
Always wear a good pair of shoes,
Eat at home because you always know what you're eating
Don't go where you're not wanted
Don't convert from being a Jew
Don't talk too much
Don't hang around with the bums in the Village
Go home,
get a Job.

Emptying the box in search of something from my mother
I realized she never learned how to write
except to sign her name and address
where they don't live anymore in Manhattan
holding my hand on the way home from the movies,
under her coat in the rain,

when I look up I can still see her face and
feel the warm hand that held me tight,
and the free comic book in my pocket

HAIR OFF THE DOG

woke up this morning good luck,
kissed his ass if he could reach
for anything but cigarettes and coffee
roll thin Golden Virginia, yeah
if he says 10 cigs a day it's more like how many, stops counting
eyes now runs after the morning news, good cheap Scotch
Old Barrister, John Glenn bottler of mental botch,
you can smell the booze

oh John, upon thee his sanity rests upon
whiskey to keep alive
proletarian ecstasy, warm belly, pronouns pinched
he's on his way to partial oblivion
of brain cells already in decay -
don't they ever get in the way?

next is breakfast, until which
4 more cigarettes were smoked to kill the hairy bitch,
plus two shots double to finish her off

Ah well, how high can you get before you forget your own name
especially after some good hash so plentiful
no one to blame for choosing a life of short pleasure
and cruising before you crash!
for a life of healthy pain
made shorter by losing…

best thing to do when you're hung over is drink some more,
she said.
will take the hair off the dog, before it's dead

BLACK TAFFETA

where does it go, all that love we had or hadn't?
to jail, to life eternal in your bottom drawer,
or hung in your closet?

or where?
oh tell us where

but no, how dare we reminisce
how gently pulled our bashful underwear,
that stolen touch
that dark forever kiss,
that torn black dress you never learned to sew
the one you wore each night
and dropped on the floor

these my friends are all our lovers past,
or present lie like ghosts between our sheets,
on pillows lie

old letters lost but never thrown away old pains,
remorse, old quarantine, decay,
old black taffeta hanging in the closet

MEMORIES OF BROOKLYN

I was there.
I could almost reach out and touch the distance,
the delicate balance between us,
between the beating heart seated there and the eyes of the man,
the becoming of…the partaking of having been in the past tense
born other than myself, wondering what I would be doing there
parked on a street corner on Kings Highway
at 4 o'clock in the morning, holding a plastic bag
with my left hand in my back pocket, at that time of day?

Another nervous me-looking lady is waiting for a bus,
her face resembles the fragile consciousness
beating in my head, which wondered only a moment ago
why it could take half a lifetime
for the price of eggs to drop 50 cents,
while the cost of everything else always seems to go up.
Strange this short distance transmigration of ethos.
do they wonder if I am as much in them as they are in me
perhaps feel the same sensitive pulse of an alien being
coursing through the veins somewhere
between the wrist and the elbow

'Are you working?'
the voice at the window of my cab inquires.
'Where you going?' (can't be too careful
nowadays) 'How much to Flatlands and 56th?'
For 6 bucks I shudder all the way at the thought
of a knife in my back,
and the hungry man climbing out of the night
into the backseat, into the perfect
environment of my rock-n-roll taxi,
a hideous monster demanding all my money,
leaving me dead for a hundred bucks
and a half-smoked pack of Camel light cigarettes

STEEPLECHASER

how to spend $3 and 58 cents in Coney Island
between 3 boys,
was my whole life one day back in1952
GEORGE C. TILYOU'S STEEPLECHASE
PAVILION OF FUN
'DON'T BE A GLOOMSTER, BE A STEEPLECHASER'

George's face like a Flying Tower out of Talmud
when the moon was a flower, and a Cyclone up the street
how sweet
3 hotdogs at Nathan's with mustard and sauerkraut,
we were the kings of Stillwell Avenue, me Joey and Irv
elbowed the crowd up to the counter,
we had a lotta nerve,

3 Cokes = minus 45 cents
which now leaves $3 and 3 cents to divvy up,
why worry when you're *inside* the Steeplechase,
on the rides

but how to choose to choose? there were so many!
the Golden Stairs,
the Bounding Billows,
the Whirlpool,
not to mention of course the Soup Bowl,
and the Electric Horse Race,
all aboard the massive billboard of George C. Tilyou's face
large as a Ferris Wheel
tall as a Parachute,
his piano teeth happy as a dime you found in your pocket
or nickel on the street

'DON'T BE A GLOOMSTER, BE A STEEPLECHASER'
buy your ticket and take your ride,
the Cave of the Winds,
the Human Billiard Table,
the Down and Out,
all the rides are inside,
oh hurry hurry, i almost forgot,
the Razzle Dazzle,
the Barrel of Love
and the Uncle Sam

(to short the story takes,
we ran out of money for the ride home
climbed up the girders to the tracks
and hopped the next train back to Manhattan)

AMERICAN WOMAN

She crosses her legs
and pulls her dress down over her knees
as she sits on the subway to Brooklyn,
reading the Old Testament.
Jesus dominates her thinking
to whom she is wedded,
an immaculate virgin
pruning herself for the new messiah.

Not only are her legs crossed but her neck,
hanging from a crucifix
reveals ever so faint
slight white patch of pale skin concealing
the mystery of her flesh.

OH MY AMERICA

oh my America,
Mozart makes me fly
but only Stephan Foster can make me cry
my Manhattah, my old black Joe
my east my west and my mid-land
from shore to shining shore,
take heart in your dreams whatever able
to put food on your table

you gave them land but the people didn't ask for land,
they asked for bread
how can every election be so close as be decided
one vote
one man
one state
and still be divided,
counting absentee ballots from the dead
where tombstones writ their names above their heads

ah well,
no better or worse in hell together
we rise again
strong families and children burning the lamp of freedom
via WiFi

BROOKLYN IS...

Brooklyn is moving from Manhattan to Parkside Avenue
circa '56, Erasmus Hall with Bobby fisher and Barbara Streisand
and Garfield's cafeteria on Ocean and Flatbush Avenues,
Brooklyn is Boro Park and Bay Ridge and Brooklyn Heights
and Linda Zuckerman and brainy Miriam Finegold
my first love my second my tenth my next to last
exit from Flatbush Billiards to Saint Marks and the Bouwerie,
Brooklyn is my dad standing by the King's Highway station
reading a newspaper he found in a garbage can around the corner
at OTB,
Brooklyn is an old phone book in pencil and spit
smudged around the edges like a halo of dust
but still readable. Oh when will those Manhattan days
and Brooklyn nights at my mother's house disappear forever?
No, never. At one time,
there were more Jews in Brooklyn than in the State of Israel,
Rheingold Beer in Williamsburg and the Brooklyn Navy Yard
where my father worked as a machinist during the war,
I still have his quaint catalog of Starret tools
he was so proud of, somewhere in a box,
Brooklyn is a day's pay for driving a taxi all night
delivering drugs like a mule to Red Hook and Brownsville
from Bedford Stuyvesant to Manhattan Beach, over the bridge
in Sheapshead Bay.

Brooklyn was the last stop to Coney Island when I was a kid
on the Lower East Side
when Hoboken was still the other side of the world,
across the ferry.

I am flying over Brooklyn now in my dreams,
they are all gone, Erica in the park and Italian pizza
at the King's Highway station.

IS THAT ALL YOU GOT?

went to fleamarket today as usual
after bombs fell in Tel Aviv last night -
about 2pm sirens went off again, 2 minutes, then Boom!
can't tell exactly where, information is spare
for good reason. don't ask. fuck you!

i recall during the Lebanese campaign
with my friend Oded up north, a rocket fired across the field.
'Wow!' i said.
'What do mean wow?
is that all you got, motherfuckers?' he shouted,
raising his fist over his head.

b'ezrat Ha Shem
we will be here tomorrow, in real-time.
bows to Emirates and opens the floodgates to hell

MIRIAM'S WELL – between the land and the sea

there went another Boom about an hour ago...
so now daily, along with my coffee the green tail parrots
and mynahs and crow, and fussy little finches
i gotta watch out for the missiles them too
revolve in the sovereignty of birds, just moved in uninvited
and a most vicious specie, a kind of man-created monstrosity
of sleek and wireless death
and you can't see the buggers flying in the sunlight!

so i walked to the sea tonight after the first Boom
because when the sirens go off
i feel oddly protected by the darkness.
also, you can see the little flares in the sky, blinking
as missiles descend in a curve of extinguishing candlelight

and i sat down and cried out to the sea, and waited
to use my magic powers to jinx the next boom to come.
i prayed to the sea to swallow all the missiles
because it doesn't hurt water when it falls. i ranted face to fate
the universe and demanded they stop the siren's falsetto,
i pled tolerance and the moral imperative
i reached into the sky with hands of friendship
until a short rainstorm came and all the lights exploded
and all the bulbs burnt out!

i'm still there watching the night and the sea,
still trying to brew my magic in a cup of restless coffee
stirring my crucible where i can see it coming,
there the last flicker of candlelight glows
between the land and the sea, electrons exploding in mid-air
an omen in the shape of a flare.

and the waves lapping in and out
and here and there to tell, that if all else fails
there is always the sea, and Miriam's well

HISTORY OF THE WARS

between that war and this ever unseasonable
a dark night follows a smoggy day
a moon not enough to be a moon but a blast
strange vapors of sexuality fill the air
with dancing in Damascus
how long will this night last
between death and death there is a pause on streets
an hysteria
briefly in the shadows
in dreams canting
war again to the shouting of cheers
hidden in a vale of abandoned lovers
the cities in ruins

…this lingering witness of a dream went rogue
battered souls wandering in gray mists
sick of it
lives cut short
families shattered
days brief memoirs, and this

may you live to never have had tomorrow
the next war,
your last kiss

WEATHER REPORT - Ceasefire

forecasted, wow!
another last night the clouds opened their maws
with thunder and lightening
the likes of which i never saw,
silence followed by another war breaks loose
this aftermath,
ethos descends into ego
decimates

our gods of nature revolt and we are no more
gods of mused poets philosophies high priests divas
desperate romantics machos closet queens antics politic
asthetic popping at seams precarious presidents papels
dopers and smokers mogels Blue Angel(s) professors
systems for sale, ancient renaissance weddingdays bastard
baroque gothic muthafuka beat punk post-moderne
thermodoo-dynamic
crumbles of ash arrows, links
can't read the small print in your
email crashed!

the mistake is better than the correction
nothing really matters any more, there goes the go
birds animals flowers' confessions, fish sacraments
heavy rain embracing, huddled in trembling leaves
there goes our 'sweating selves and worse'
there is a G-d but has no name
of whom bereaved

man,
this storm in the Garden of Eden doesn't let up!
(doesn't stop my Eve from baked her peanut buttercups,
just now...)

NIGHT BEFORE LAST in Tel Aviv

The night before last, Lois and I decided to go out to dinner between the booms! tired of cooking smoking indoors pacing between bomb shelter and tv, between the sirens and the silence counting seconds, we strolled up to Yermiyahu street and stopped for something to eat. No sooner, the sirens started wailing again, we rushed into the falafel kitchen of the restaurant as many could fit, between the plates and utensils and dishpans stacked like pita breads piled up, getting ready to toast

Momentarily, among men mostly, a young girl rushed in and fell into my arms, trembling. I put my arm about her and held her saying, in Hebrew, 'Alti dag mami, h'yeh b'sedar' it will be all right, it will all be okay.

The poor child was trembling like a cliché on the news, a leaf about to fall, ran into the arms of her father and mother there, and we just stood huddled glowing quietly, half in prayer, half in wonder how long it will be to drop that bomb here, or b'ezrat ha'shem, G-d willing, into the sea where it can't hurt anyone. It was all somewhere up there in some alien ionosphere or evil destiny, what did it matter which just how far is it falling distance from us poor souls standing here. I felt like the ghost of a camera recoiled, ready to shoot incoming atrocities...such black and white at night, is stilled.

On our way home we looked at the fashions in shop windows on Dizengoff. Lois' little face lit up! I said 'You know, if every time a bomb falls a pretty girl rushes into my arms, well hey, let them fall, give it all you got. ha!...because we were truly blessed having been there already passed, if only to comfort her and all our children. We both laughed heartily. We are all one, after all, whether we rise or fall. And if i'm to die, i want to die at home. If my children were born into my arms, then it will be into their arms i must fall. It will then be for them to decide their way home...

HOLD ON

the strings that bind between us are stretched to snapping!
don't let go of your love when it falls
look at a wave comes back to shore
look at poor Poe for his lost Lenore
look at the nest last spring was made
look at the sun in the shade
and the shade in the sun
hear the gentle birds hum, as before

after the storm
celebrate the norm
and when they break, and they will again
and the sirens wail as before their booms
and the waves wash out to sea
remember the arms that held you tight
remember those missiles that flew at night
remember the candles burning brightly
remember your home in desperate ruin
remember the roof that covered your head
remember the bread left on your table
remember the stark and lonely room…

remember the soldiers now dead
held on as were able

and though we pray to be heard as hell rages
bless the silence,
holiest

IT ALL GOES ROUND IN MY HEAD

LOIS MICHAL UNGER

Selected Poems

Dedication

For my Mother

ACKNOWLEDGEMENTS

Some of these poems have been published in the San Gabriel Valley Poetry Quarterly, Maggid, Iton 77, Guerilla Pamphlet, Real Stories Gallery, Deronda Review, Poetry Repairs, The Glass Lies Shattered All Around and The Apple of His Eye.

CONTENTS/Indices

INTRODUCTION

Sometimes there's something attractive about dirty. I took off my sleeveless undershirt, folded it and put it away, not in the hamper. It wasn't dirty really, just old and grey like when you've washed white too many times. It felt sexy. Made me think of the time I was on a bus from Missouri to Texas, when I was in a children's theatre company. It was a two day trip. I couldn't sleep and stayed up reading Emile Zola's 'Nana'. There's a scene when Nana and her friend Satin are sitting on a bed, talking. Nana is the successful rich courtesan and Satin is a street waif. She's wearing a dirty slip. I was 18 and I've always remembered that.

JUDY GARLAND'S FACE AND HER HANDS

It happened at the lunch counter at Macy's
where the Christmas hired actors ate
A girl announced she wanted to play Marjorie Morningstar
You're too sensitive for that said a boy

Somehow she ended up at Columbia Pictures
doing a modeling job for 'A Star is Born'
it would be Judy Garland's face and her body on the billboard

She had the flu that day but went anyhow
in a blue shirt and tights in the lights
her hands held close to her face

In the end they used Judy Garland's face and her hands

the picture of her hands and Judy Garland's face
in a box
her children could see as she washed dishes or dried dishes
or changed diapers
hey mom
there's a picture of Judy Garland with your hands!

THE NITE OF A POETRY READING
AT KHATCHORPURI RESTAURANT (for M.R)

I don't think of you often
but today I'll think of you
standing aloof in black pants and white shirt at the counter
in the paper it said you died of an overdose
I don't believe it – never knew you to take drugs
still, you wore long sleeve shirts

I died in your bed of an overdose
no that's all wrong
I took four seconals and went to sleep in your bed
when you woke me up you said you're fired
I thought that skuzzy of you
to treat me like hired help
and not your girlfriend
we were in touch a little bit after that
but you went back to your wife
I fell in love and got married

He went to your restaurant sometimes
I mentioned that I knew you

ARTIE WALDORF

I was 9 when Artie Waldorf got out of prison
and grabbed my mother and kissed her
I know he just got out because
my sister stayed up late and listened

That winter his wife Frances wore lots of jewelry
                              and mink coats
his son Jacky gave me my first kiss

Once he put his fist through my mother's dumbwaiter
when my uncle Sammy's friend Cream Cheese
came on to Frances

It was the winter Frances wore all the jewelry
                              and mink coats
or maybe it was the next one
that Artie got shot to death in a barbershop chair

Daddy said he probably wanted too much.

DE.TE.RI.O.RATE :
To grow worse in quality or state

One could deteriorate slowly
like
not picking up crumbs
or
bottles
or sweeping gathered dust
feathers under the bed
tissues
unpolished boots
could lie around
clothes left on chairs
one could deteriorate
slowly
not even perked
up
by a change in the
weather

UNTITLED

Her leg was pushed apart
brusquely
by his knee
she was there
under him,
there wasn't one
moment he seemed
to consider her.
Isn't there someone
I can take, she thought
who'll be nice to me
with just a cruel edge?

THEY BOTH CAME TO BREAKFAST WITH ME

They both came to breakfast with me
sat across the table from my coffee
I couldn't depend on either of them anymore
See, I told you you were strong
the dead one said.

I WAS READY FOR REDEMPTION

I was ready for redemption
that nite
and all the other nites
of my new love

my old love was loose with me
slipping me in and out of his hands

my new love held me and wouldn't let go
so tight it hurt me
turned my face to face his

IT ALL GOES ROUND IN MY HEAD

when I drink a glass of wine
it all goes round in my head
lines from plays I've been in
plays I loved
'I shot a man in San Francisco once'
'Lakme Productions presents The Way We Live'
it goes round in my head
and people I've known
some of them dead
and places I've been
and places I've been

when the tension begins to build
I need a glass of wine

and places I've been

Lakme Productions presents The Way We Live
brought to you by Libby, Mac Neil and Libby
but that wasn't so
it was My True Story on the radio
brought to you by Libby, Mac Neil and Libby

I listened in daddy's scratchy chair
when I stayed home from school
I hated school
was afraid of the old Irish Catholic teachers
with purple and blue hair.
sometimes I pretended to have fun
like when I picked out the see-through nitegown
to give the teacher on Christmas

she didn't like it
it was movie star material
Lakme Productions presents The Way We Live

it all goes round in my head

THE CLIENT DOES NOT OWN THE RIGHTS

She wore a black taffeta dress for the picture
hair dyed black
cigarette hanging out of her mouth

she was drunk she forgot her name

the taffeta smelled from sweat
her dress sewn tight
the cigarette felt like her only friend

her picture is in a museum
she long forgotten
hair no longer black

still her picture hangs in a museum

FOR GEORGE KESSLERE

I was only eighteen when I met you
I thought you lived in a museum
when I posed for you
when you painted me
then we both knew what we were doing.

WHERE KINGS ONCE WALKED

I'm not interested in planets
speed of lights away
want to know whether King David saw the same sky as me
what Rachel wore to the wedding feast

Was the sky different three thousand years ago

In the harbor soft waves lap
against the boardwalk
fishermen cast poles
where there's a restaurant
a king once walked

LIKE A FIG

He said you look like a fig
and I knew there was some memory
something revealed in a similar conversation
another time

it wasn't Columbia or Broadway
no it wasn't that

his face looked round and baby face
when he said you look like a fig
tenderly

I tried to reach for the memory
of what it reminded me
and hung up a skirt

A HAPPY ENDING

the movie was not going to have a happy ending
I could tell that
the girl was not going to clean up
stop taking drugs
so I got up and left

POEMS ABOUT YOU

He said, you don't write poems about me
and I looked at his baby face
I thought of the everyday things we share
and the life in palaces
and caves with electric lights
no, I said, I guess I don't write poems about you

BROKEN SLATS

Broken slats across the way
hiding what broken dreams
what broken conquests
an old man getting up at 4 a.m.
waking me with the clatter of his walker
I know nothing about him
just that I peek at him
thru the slats
at 4 a.m.
clattering down the street

YELLOW CAR

He was like a stopper for her
and yet he admired cars that went full blast
sometimes she turned the motor on in the dark
in his drunken days he never noticed which car she drove
now sober he did

she bought a yellow number
a car that is
decorated it with blue
and wondered what to do next

SEE THROUGH PAJAMAS

Life slips by
like see through pajamas,
a sheer nightgown

you call your friend long distance
no answer just a machine
once – twice

my cousin I call
too early – leave a message

dead lovers gone
scenes and moments remembered
you don't put a name to these sentences
you see them in your mind,
readers use their imagination

but I remember so much
wonder why life goes by
like a see through pajama

I FELL IN LOVE WITH YOU

I fell in love with you
when I read your Poem to the Motherfucker
men are animals to me
who know how to fix things
the rest is playing house

it burnt in the fire
I just remember the title now

THE OTHER SIDE OF WEST BROADWAY

West Broadway – we went to a party
in a loft where a rock band lived
we're going to move in with them you told my family
my mother looked at you in horror
it was your fantasy for the day
she thought it was real
it wasn't a fantasy or real for me
we had taken our baby to the party

I saw them feed their cat
on the rug – no plate
No way would I move in
why didn't I tell my mother that?
maybe I did

West Broadway –
streets Edgar Allen Poe once walked

I lost my family
on West Broadway
in your oo-la-la
and cloud of smoke

IN THE PHOTOGRAPHER'S STUDIO

in the photographer's studio
I'm bathed with light
I wear more clothes or less clothes
later I become religious
my family complains about my clothes

it's afternoon
my husband focuses his camera
my back hurts
outside hammer sounds
air blowing thru the window
sways the curtains

WIFE ACCUSED

what are you writing – dreams
his voice edges at me
and i darting between the raindrops reply no
with the right lightness measured in my words.
wife accused
and i darting between the raindrops of my words

FLEE MARKET

I come here he said
to hold back the loneliness
she understands
he touches two of her posters
the two recent ones
their eyes meet
his hair is grey
as he walks away
she thinks
he touched the one
I just bought
that I wasn't sure of.

A POETRY READING IN THE CARMEL SHUK

You're breaking my heart he said
surrounded by fish and olives in the Carmel Shuk.
Why don't you buy here anymore?

She's breaking my heart he said

Well, I bought canned beans
and when you put the cans in the bag it smelled of fish
and I didn't like that

She didn't even mention the dead mouse her daughter had seen
So she walked a ways, went to the poetry reading
and opened up her blank notebook

I SAW JERRY AT THE SHUK

I saw Jerry at the Shuk
I come here
he said
sometimes if I'm feeling lonely
or need a lift
it's so lively

we stood on a corner talking
and I thought
I have to go
but really what's the rush?

did you dye your hair
or is it a wig?
it looks nice
he said

FIRST LIPSTICK

Little sisters are the ones,
they can never forget
conversations in the dark
across twin beds

sisters tell secrets
scream in the nite in future years
and nobody knows why

a half century later
she remembers
her sister's first lipstick –
fatal apple
by Revlon

HE TOLD MY HUSBAND

He told my husband I was a fool and had no discretion
I wish I could smack his face and claw his skin off.

'Mommy, I'm not doing so well,
I sent a bill to the wrong company.
See mama, I just want to see him once more
to see his soft eyes on me.
I took two poems out of my book that could embarrass him
and he'll never know'

'You're not the only person who keeps secrets'

'But it hurts'

'So does my old age. I wake up every day and
wonder if it will be the last.'

I STAND ON THE SHORE

I stand on the shore for a visit
the wind has died down
I begin counting time
the scrape of a car tire on gravel
steps on the staircase
all of it done before.

EYE SHADOW (for Alicia)

girls splash eye shadow in the spring
after long winter underwear and sweaters
blue skirts red skirts white yellow
smile at the reflection in the mirror
girls splash eye shadow in the spring

BOAT

The boat was dashed in pieces,
still the water had a nice salty taste
as she walked along the wreckage
licking her fingers

the sun shone
she kicked the water along the boards
touching the boat here and there.

HARRY

Harry played piano on a Saturday nite
asked a chorus girl out

he's a junky the dance captain said

that chorus girl she's afraid
she dont wanna walk too close to Harry

'fraid he'd stick her with something
an she be a junky too

Harry just wanna jam in a niteclub
his big hands died along with him in the winter
of an overdose

THINGS THAT GO BUMP IN THE NITE

1964 – Tyrone Guthrie Theatre

MOLLIE SCHOP 1924

TOYS IN THE BASEMENT

The baby called to me from the cellar
where old toys were kept
I heard a melody a child's song
I told them I heard it
and they said it was only a toy

I was sorry for what I'd done
when I woke up I knew it was murder

I tried to replace you after you were gone
that's when I heard the toys in the basement
and they said it wasn't you
There's a picture of me from that period
when I became pregnant again
I look so happy,
but I bled one night into my long winter underwear

Then we were in Arizona
I remember that time in pastel colors
I wore maternity clothes right away
We took a walk in the desert
that nite you were gone again
in the hospital I cried
wrote a letter to my mother,
I tried to find G-d's forgiveness

In Vermont
we took walks in the woods
you came back again

G-d forgave me
G-d blessed me
G-d shone His light on me

I found a baby in my stomach
it was you

DRIVING A HARD BARGAIN

Driving a hard bargain
acting out your fantasies
pioneer woman
with Indian braids
no diaphragm is
sexual freedom
is love on a bed
without coils or pills
is no
restraint
and another baby in the hills.

It's because of the pain
that I can't enjoy the exquisite scenery
the fatigue around my eyes
dulls
the crisp air
the white snow
the spruce huddling together.

TOMATIE RED

tomatie red mama told me
is a good color on dismal days
mama and friends playing mah jong
i in bed listening to the stillness
then mah jong ring out
sound of tiles clicking
sound of mah jong

sound of ice cream on second avenue
sound of second avenue el
drunks sleeping underneath
grandma and grandpa grocery store
early morning
grandpa setting up the stand

rockaway cold water
mama and sisters in bathing suits
pot of food

now i wear tomatie red in my own life
not little girl watching
i teach grandchildren play hide the beans
and sing songs mama sang

no aunt with spumoni nickels
ice cream truck come around soon
grandson ask me for and run down

WOMAN IN RED

She waits every day for the lover
who said he'd come back to her
forty years ago

She waits in front of the house
always in a red shirt
'I'll be wearing red' she told him

New neighbors have moved in
new eyes peer out of their kitchen window

I'll wait one more time she tells herself,
maybe the army called him
maybe a work problem came up

Soon the waiting itself is a ritual
and one year one day
she waits not knowing why

AT THAT MOMENT OF LEAVING

At that moment of leaving
when you read a magazine
as if it would go on
continue
be back again
And I knew
suspected you wouldn't
it wouldn't

I wanted to hold that moment
keep that moment
I had to let go and say goodbye

MUMMY HEAD – A MOVIE SCRIPT

the mummies that got smashed
take revenge

looters found dead
headlines scream
innocent guys with big dreams

in the hotel where my daughter once stayed in Taba
an actor sits at a bar
blonde girl joins him
she's a file clerk,
but got the idea
the looters were killed by the mummies!

it's one of these mysteries
that doesn't really get solved

the truth lies somewhere
in mysterious elements

maybe in the Sinai desert
the tinkle of donkey bells

a seemingly quiet day
a mummy rises
puts his head back on
walks out of the museum

PEACE IN THE MIDDLE EAST

I'll give you peace
say our enemies
just give me your neck
so I can choke it.

MEETINGS

Shall I say it,
I was in New Mexico
you were in Jerusalem
we didn't meet
it wasn't our time to meet

Outside there's a big tree
birds sit on the top branch
sometimes parrots
sometimes mynah birds
some signal passes between them
whose turn it is

If we had been meant to meet
I would have travelled to Jerusalem
the day you were there
or you would have traveled to Rudioso

The thing about believing in G-d is
it's all in His hands
with a little leeway

DIDN'T WE KNOW

Didn't we know when we wore black dresses
and ran through Saks Fifth Avenue
that it would all come to nothing.

When you held me close in your trench coat
kissed me then spun away
you didn't know
what came after would come to nothing.

We didn't know any of it
I'm going to live to be very old
and my memories will fade.

MY MOTHER WAS A FLAPPER

The stories my mother told me
were my mother's milk

she went dancing at the Cotton Club
she was a flapper
a rich man wanted to marry her
but she preferred my father
her parents bought her sister a fur coat
and her an imitation
so she put her coat on the clothesline
and set it on fire
she stabbed her brother
when he took her potatoes

I know my mother's stories
they were my mother's milk

INSOMNIA

Tiredness old friend for one reason or another
gripping me up
I have tried all my life to find order
it's always on its way
'just make a decision' he said
'one way or the other
and stick to it'

In the universe of things
I'm a slip
a strand of hair in time
the trees are brown too
only time is supreme.

BEFORE YOUR TRIP

I danced the last waltz with you before you left us
building by building, stone by stone they'll reclaim the city
the children will reclaim the city

the truth lies in the heap of it all
in the jungle debris of life,
when you're young you think
the time you live in is so wise,
grandparents read old newspapers lying in the street

I see it now
in the heap of things
the yellow fragment of a newspaper
linking the hands that have touched it.

you are frightened before your trip
and I say smugly, don't be frightened
as if you had nothing to be frightened about
and, rather, I should say think of hands linking
think of hands touching
and since that is so
what is there to be frightened about.

STREETS OF LOWER MANHATTAN
(after Hurricane Sandy)

streets don't remember who lived there
rain pelts down
water washes from the river
or maybe they do
generations come and gone
walking the streets of lower Manhattan

IN THE PICTURE

In the picture the people are smiling
stand before a blank wall
and what else
are there dirty dishes in the sink
garbage to throw out
how many lovers has she had
how many he had
do they intrude in dreams

In former times people
threw garbage out the window
we frown on that
it's dirty, unclean

they stand before a blank wall
holding hands

SLID IT ONTO A PLATE

She told the famous movie actress
that he roughed her up
Is it part of sex play
the actress asked

The young girl looked puzzled
she didn't really know

The actress cooked an egg
and slid it onto a plate

Even if you're just cooking
for yourself
you have to set the table elegantly
she told the young neophyte

SUICIDE BOMBER AT THE SEAPORT

he asked the man for a drink of water
their eyes must have met
then the suicide bomber
pressed the button
and blew them both up

THINGS THAT GO BUMP IN THE NITE

We passed through a good period I said
but now it's over
I hear the clanging of train wheels
the spokes make a grinding sound
I hear the sounds
of things that go bump in the nite
I remember the time I ran away from my mother
on the trolley car.

THINGS PEOPLE SAID TO ME

You're strong
the first time he yells at her children he'll be back on your doorstep
there's other fish in the sea
go out have a good time
fall in love again

These are things people say. I think they believe them

Now that I'm single again I take books to bed
spare socks in case I get cold
I say I'm going to listen to the News
but I'm too tired
listen to the gurgle of the washing machine instead

What will it be like for her
coming home
this time without daddy
she didn't come all those years
because of childhood memories of daddy
or was it grownup fight with daddy?

Outside there's a wind storm the color of hay
and rolling hills of sand
on the way to the shuk there was a bomb scare
on television a man is crying because his wife is dead

he said why did you initiate divorce proceedings
without telling me
which question to answer there were two

I initiated divorce proceedings because at a certain point
you seemed to belong more to her than to me

in the street we'd meet and the feelings between us were tender
like a boy and a girl with something to say

but after the divorce began my lawyer said
don't talk to him anymore

AFTER THE DOG WAS GONE

it was quiet nites after the dog was gone
a major scandal
like the loss of a husband

upstairs and downstairs he ran

the dogs fought
smell of death

the owner of the other dog screaming
finally
I attached the leash
to the ring around Regal's neck
the dogs could have bitten me

I had nightmares about it long after

on Purim we waited for the parade

I was afraid to be alone in the house with the dog
was the one who made the phone call to the City

SEEING YOU IN THE STORE ZEROXING
YOUR PAGES

I

Seeing you in the store zeroxing your pages
me buying envelopes
we say hello casually
my heart is beating

the children say we didn't have a good marriage
I say we did
but you grew tired of me
found another cunt more desirable
I'm happy I love you
I know this seeing you zeroxing pages in the store
there were other men I loved
but you led me down a path to home,
to mommy and daddy, to normal

I understand it all now
sometimes I see you and feel we could walk in the meadow
holding hands
I feel we could walk in the meadow holding hands fiercely
when we were only children dancing in the woods

when you delighted in my body's song
and I held a bag of riches
that was long ago and now is now
I walked out when you began talking about us
cancel the court date you said

and I reached into my pocket book took out 10 shekels
and left
the answer stuffed and smoldering inside me

II

your voice is oily sweet on the phone
selling me fish
asking polite questions
what was the Torah portion today?
I hear the oily sweet
and know something is not right

I called you Mr. get drunk in the morning
told you I'd tell her husband about your past
afterwards didn't feel good, no victory
you told our daughter you're going to marry her
nothing I say can combat that
I have to tear away your memory
sit shiva for you

the boy I knew is no more
poetry read in front of French windows
steaks from Tads steak house
showing off to me at a pool table

the boy I knew is a man with an ugly haircut
cut by his girlfriend

TUBAL-CAIN

saw him again in New York
in a place where I didn't expect to see him
Tubal-Cain
empty
raincoat
dark
at night on the telephone
I agree,
something makes me afraid
and I run out

BOOK OF PSALMS

with the boldness of a young dancer
or a hip-hop punk
tapping out the rhythm of a song
David waits for me on my bed
how come you're so comfortable in my century
i ask him
David flashes the smile that made him famous
a red haired Jimmy Dean
he offers to play on his lyre or a homemade instrument.
my light bulb needs fixing i ask him to do it.
being a poet or a king are great things
but what men really have to do is fix
my legs are so cool on the sheet
pick me up David says
i do

IT'S BEGINNING AGAIN

It's beginning again
with someone new
hands streaked with paint on my skin
I think of you and wonder how I can begin again
with someone new.

THE FOURTH TANK

he was in the fourth tank in the third row
moving up the road slowly

suddenly large metal birds appeared in the sky
with noise

zooming towards him
he didn't feel much pain
but all at once
darkness surrounded him
he was surprised

his friend in the third tank in the second row
said the country

that sent these Tomahawks
was going home today

he thought of the girl
his father picked out for him to marry
next month

he closed his eyes
wondering

if she would marry someone else

HORSES MIDSTREAM

It was only years later that she reacted to men walking
       on the moon,
when it happened she heard the news but it didn't
       mean so much
years later she thought about it and understood,
she could lay back in bed sometimes and feel the sadness
       of the growing old of people
       the growing up of the whole human race,
she remembered the clip clop of horses
       on pavement
       and horseshit
and now so clean, men on the moon.

2

Loving sometimes is the freedom to say I don't love you
loving is the freedom not to love
so the time rolls round when you love again
       with all the clatter of a lifetime.

I love you she said, in her wedding dress
the children banged pots and pans
the years clattered
there was dissention and disappointment

In the morning they hung the flag out
and said,
       when their fingers touched
       doing something together
       I still love you

3 IN THE MORNING

he snores and says did I wake you
I'm awake
it's 3 in the morning
my husband and son are home
I make coffee
eat cake
no more conversations with people
about divorce
I see a blue and white tablecloth
my white gold ring with blue sapphires
pink teapot
strainer/towel
it's 3 in the morning
dark
G-d's fingers made the stars
the refrigerator lumps along heavily

ALWAYS

you say you love me and will always
be there for me

why would you.
worries eat at me

last night someone called
who came around when you weren't here,

in the darkness night enfolded
birds and flower slept

trees stood quiet,
earlier brought lites of the reception
people greeting

and delicate cakes

AFTER THE DREAM

after the dream
I walked in the street
slow motion
melodies in my head
songs
slow motion
and perfume

after the dream
the light from the cell phone blinked

I LOVE YOU SILENTLY

I love you silently
when you return late at nite
in darkened rooms
cats crying outside
hear your footsteps
and babies

A FULL DAY

a full day is standing at the sink washing dishes
watching birds fly overhead
flying to where they're going
the trick in life is not to know all the answers
sunlight covering everything
and the trees

ABOUT THE AUTHORS

E.L. Freifeld

Born April 15, 1941 in Manhattan, of Jewish immigrants from Poland and Galicia, Elazar spans two literary generations from the streets of New York to Tel Aviv. His poems and stories have appeared in numerous books, literary magazines, newspapers and anthologies throughout the world.

Since first publishing in 1964, he has had 15 books published, including The Importance of Swimming, Television Analogs, Love Cycles, A Jew in the House of Harvard, Poet's Guide to the Holy Land, The World According to Animals and What Walks.

A Jew in the House of Harvard was awarded first prize by the Israel Federation of Writers for the year 1987. Translated into 8 languages, including Hebrew, French, Spanish, Italian, Russian, Turkish and Hungarian, Elazar's readings and seminars include such venues as,

The New School for Social Research, The Whitney Museum School of American Art, WBAI Radio, WNET TV/Channel 13, CBS TV/Video at The School of Visual Arts, and the American Embassy in Tel Aviv.

During the Scud War in Israel, continuing a career begun in the U.S., Elazar wrote a weekly column for The Jerusalem Post and is now contributing editor of LeConte Publications, in Rome. When asked to comment on his own work, he says; 'Every poem and story I write is like the first poem or story I ever wrote'.

Lois Michal Unger

Lois Michal Unger was born in New York City. She was an actress before becoming a poet and appeared in plays on and off Broadway including The Diary of Anne Frank, Things That Go Bump In The Nite and The Red Shoes. She got married and the family moved to Vermont in 1970, grew food and lived without electricity for five years. In 1982, she moved to Israel with her husband and three children and now lives in Tel Aviv.

About writing in general and poetry in particular she has this to say. "As a child I wrote poetry and won a prize from Junior Scholastic Magazine. Then I became an actress. Then I got married. When we moved to Vermont, I began writing again. From the start I had my own way of putting things, my own voice. Sometimes I'm guided by Jack Kerouac's remark: 'First thought best thought.' My best poems write themselves and I'm just the vehicle.